W9-CDL-122

MEGA WHEELS

Designer: Paul Calver
Written and edited by: Christiane Gunzi
Editorial assistant: Katy Rayner
Vehicle consultant: Gary Boyd-Hope

an imprint of
SCHOLASTIC

This edition published by Tangerine Press, an imprint of Scholastic Inc., 557 Broadway; New York, NY 10012

10 9 8 7 6 5 4 3 2 1

ISBN-10: 0-545-00047-5
ISBN-13: 978-0-545-00047-5

Printed & bound in China

CONTENTS

SPORTS CARS

These fast, exciting cars are sports cars. They are low on the ground and they have space for two people. The Lamborghini Murciélago is named after a Spanish bull that was famous for being brave and strong. Sports cars cost a lot of money.

Ferrari F430

Ferrari

This Italian car has a gearbox like Formula One racing cars, so the driver can change gears very quickly.

Lamborghini

This sports car has a top speed of 211 miles (339 km) an hour. It has long wing mirrors which can fold in and out.

Inside a Lamborghini

Porsche

This German car can go from 0 to 60 miles an hour in four seconds. It has excellent brakes, so it can stop suddenly when it needs to.

SUPERCARS

Some sports cars are so fast and fantastic that only the richest people in the world can afford to buy them. These beautifully-designed supercars take a very long time to make. One supercar can cost more than a house.

Can you point to?

wheel

headlights

logo

Bugatti Veyron

Koenigsegg CCX

Koenigsegg

In 2005, a Koenigsegg supercar won the world record for being the fastest production car. It raced at 241 miles (387 km) an hour.

How many McLaren F1 supercars are there?

Bugatti

This is one of the most expensive cars in the world. It is built by hand, and it takes 1,200 people to make one single car.

McLaren F1

McLaren

Only 107 McLaren F1 supercars have ever been made. They were built between 1994 and 1998. These cars have lots of power but they are light in weight. Their top speed is 240 miles (386 km) an hour.

Bugatti Veyron racing along

LUXURY CARS

Prime ministers, presidents, and royal families travel in big, luxury cars. These cars are comfortable, powerful, and smart. A Rolls-Royce can carry 26 gallons (100 liters) of fuel in its tank, so it can drive for 400 miles (643 km) without stopping for fuel.

Chrysler 300C Saloon

Chrysler

The Chrysler has a 425 horsepower engine. This means that its engine has as much power as 425 horses if they were pulling the car along!

Mercedes CLK55 AMG

Mercedes

This powerful car can go from 0 to 62 miles (0 to 99 km) an hour in five seconds. It goes up to 155 miles (249 km) an hour. It has two exhaust pipes, and heated electric mirrors that fold in and out.

Can you point to?

logo

steering wheel

grille

Maybach

This luxury German two-seater has wider tires than most cars. It looks like a sports car from the 1930s.

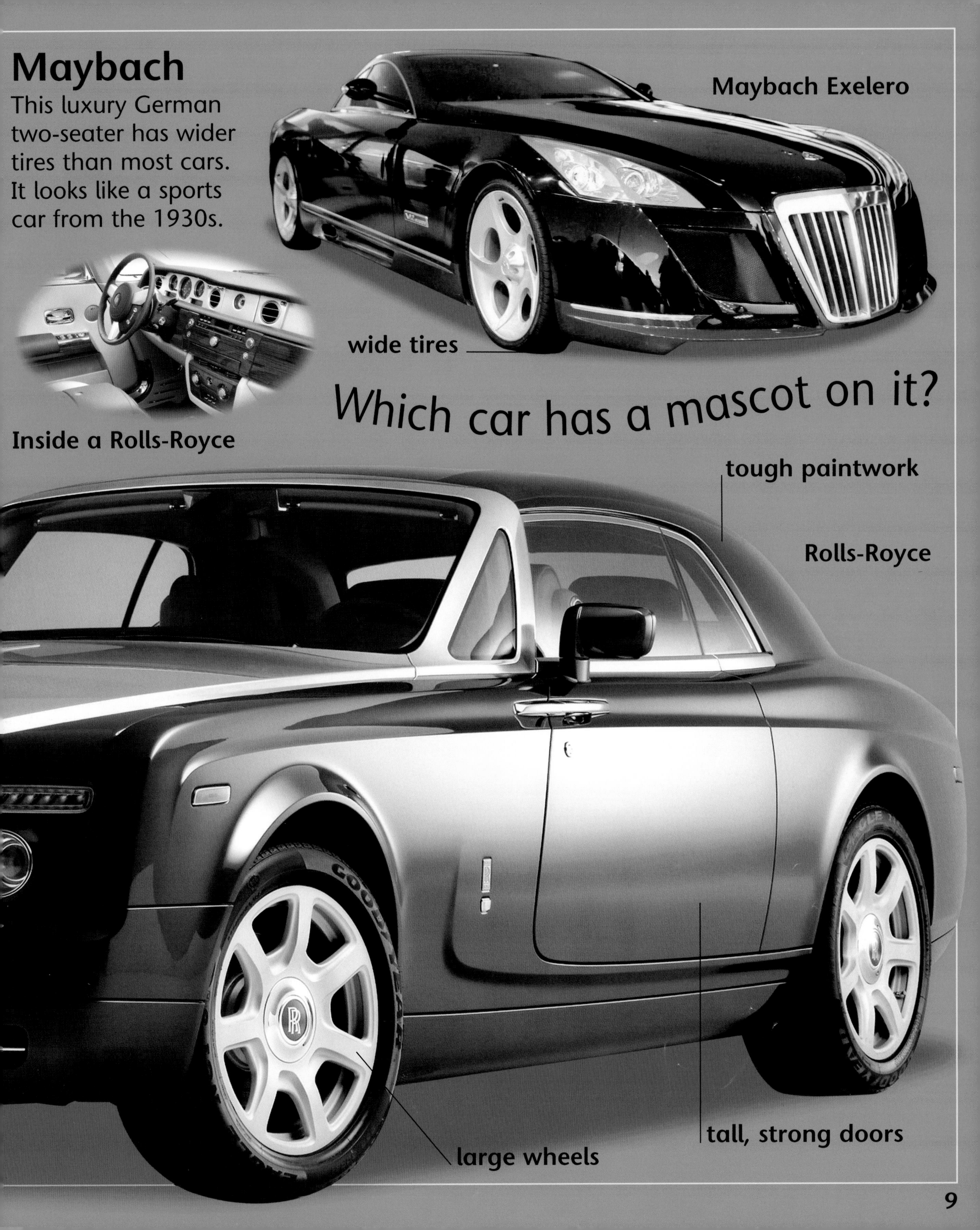

RACE AND RALLY CARS

Race and rally cars are normal road cars specially made with powerful engines and gears. People race them on roads and on muddy tracks in all sorts of weather. Rally drivers are some of the best drivers in the world.

Ford Focus

Ford

This Ford Focus rally car has a four-cylinder turbo-charged engine.

Which rally car has a turbo-charged engine?

rear spoiler

Porsche RS Spyder

Aston Martin

This British two-seater Aston Martin sports car is built by hand. It has a 600 horsepower V12 engine, and it can go up to 220 miles (354 km) an hour.

Aston Martin Vanquish

Dodge

The Dodge rally car can race along at up to 230 miles (370 km) an hour. This car is driven in the famous NASCAR races in America and Canada.

Dodge R/T

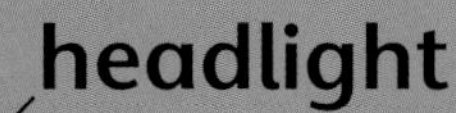

headlight

Porsche

The exciting Porsche RS Spyder can go from 0 to 60 miles (0 to 96 km) an hour in three seconds. This car drove in the Le Mans race in America. The Le Mans race is 24 hours long.

front spoiler

air intake

FORMULA ONE CARS

Motor racing is a fast, dangerous sport. Formula One cars race in competitions around the world called Grand Prix, which means "big prize." These cars cost millions of dollars to build. There is huge prize money for the winner.

The Grand Prix

In a Grand Prix race, the cars have to race each other around a track.

BMW Sauber

This is Canadian driver Jacques Villeneuve in a Sauber. The car has a BMW engine and Michelin tires.

McLaren Mercedes

This McLaren has Michelin tires and a Mercedes engine. The driver is Kimi Raikkonen of Finland.

Renault

This French car is made by Renault. The driver is Fernando Alonso of Spain. He is the youngest Formula One champion in the world.

Where are Formula One Ferraris made?

Ferrari

Michael Schumacher's Ferrari was made in Italy by the Ferrari team. This car has Bridgestone tires.

DRAGSTERS AND HOT RODS

Hot rods are built out of old cars and painted bright colors. Fat tires and a bigger engine are added, then people race their cars on tracks. Drag racing is when two dragsters race each other on a short, straight track. Drag racing is exciting to watch.

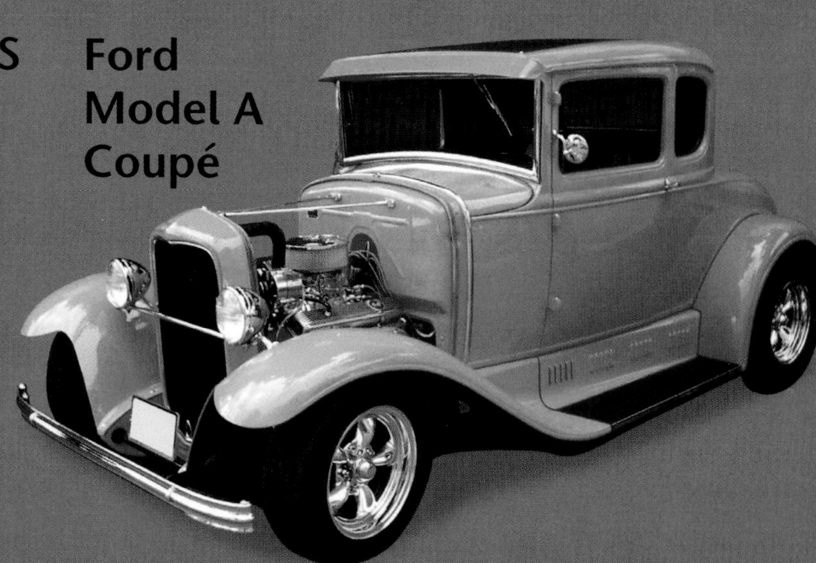

Ford Model A Coupé

Ford

The first hot rods were built out of old Ford cars. You can see the engine inside this one.

1966 Chevrolet Chevelle SS

Chevrolet

This colorful car was made in 1966 and it has been painted red with flames on the bonnet.

Fuel Altered Dragster

Can you point to?

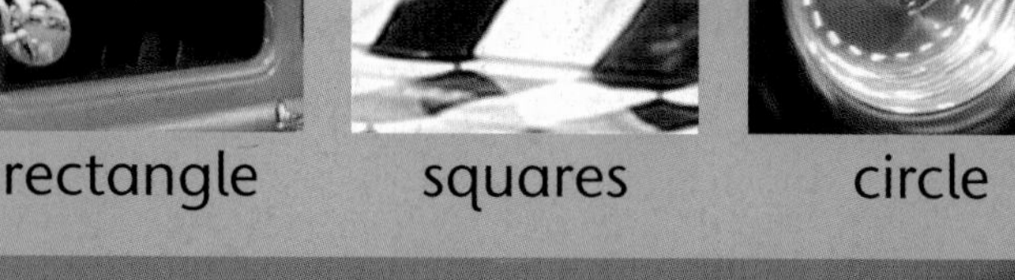

rectangle squares circle

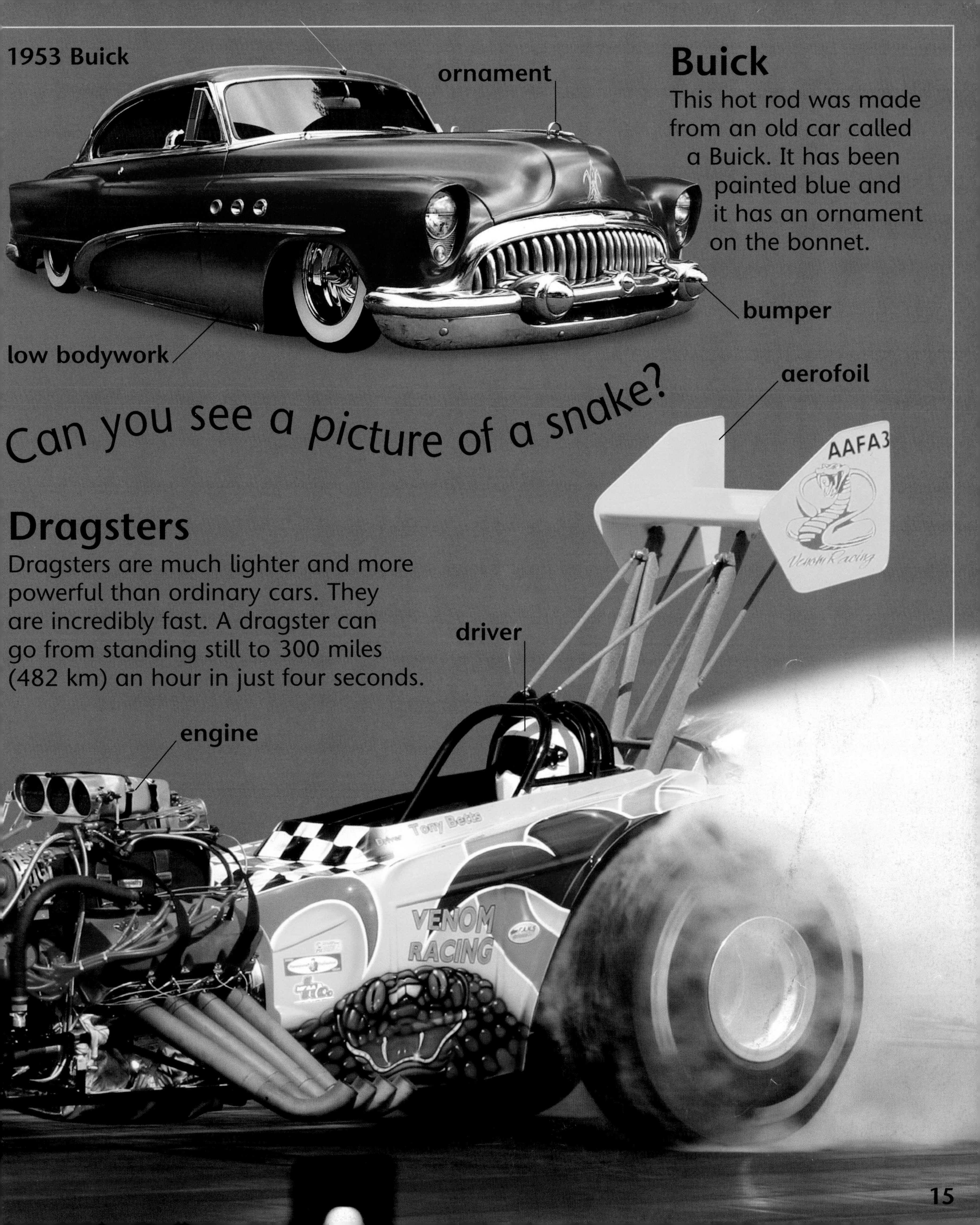

Buick

This hot rod was made from an old car called a Buick. It has been painted blue and it has an ornament on the bonnet.

Can you see a picture of a snake?

Dragsters

Dragsters are much lighter and more powerful than ordinary cars. They are incredibly fast. A dragster can go from standing still to 300 miles (482 km) an hour in just four seconds.

FOUR-BY-FOURS

These big, strong vehicles are driven along by all four wheels at the same time. Four-by-fours can easily climb up steep slopes, drive through mud, and pull heavy loads. These powerful vehicles are often used on farms.

Can you point to?

lights

grille guard

spare wheel

What colors are these four-by-fours?

Hummer

These cars have big chrome grille guards at the front. On the bumper there are strong metal loops for pulling things along.

Land Rover

Four-by-fours are so tough and well built that they can drive through water without damaging the engine. The driver sits high up, away from the ground.

A good grip

Jeeps, Land Rovers, and Hummers have powerful engines. They can drive over rocks, mud, ice, and snow and up steep mountain tracks without sliding around.

PICK-UPS

These big, powerful pick-up trucks are used by farmers and builders to do tough jobs. They can carry heavy loads and tow other vehicles. People also like to use pick-up trucks because they are fun to drive.

Ford F750

Ford F650

This Ford pick-up has a 300 horsepower engine. Some Fords have a special camera that helps the driver see behind the vehicle when it is towing things.

Ford F650

Dodge Ram

This fast pick-up can go from 0 to 60 miles (0 to 96 km) an hour in five seconds. Its top speed is 154 miles (247 km) an hour and it has a 500 horsepower engine.

Which pick-up is called the Dodge M80?

Ford F950

Can you point to?

exhaust

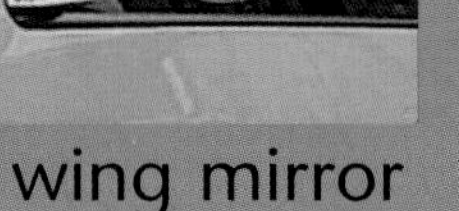
wing mirror

wheel arch

Dodge M80

Dodge M80

This cool pick-up looks like a truck from the 1930s. It is strong and it has five gears. Dodge pick-ups are tough machines and can drive over rough ground.

MONSTER TRUCKS

About 30 years ago, a few people decided to make their pick-ups look more exciting. They added huge wheels and their trucks were called "monster trucks." Now millions of people watch these mega vehicles race and do displays at shows.

Can you point to?

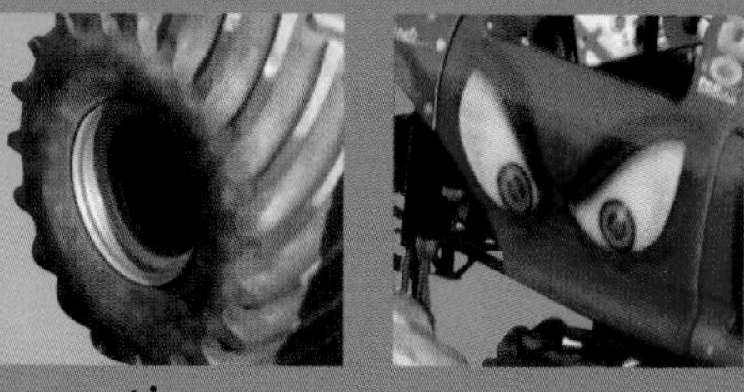

tire eyes teeth

Bigfoot

The owner of the first monster truck, "Bigfoot," added huge tires to his Ford truck then drove over some old cars in a field for fun.

Clever tricks

Drivers make their trucks do jumps. Some spin their truck in a circle. This is called a "doughnut."

Which was the first monster truck?

"Monstrous"

"Swamp Thing"

Car crusher

Monster trucks race each other, jump and crush other vehicles by driving over them. They have special switches that turn off the engine if the driver loses control.

FUN CARS

Some cars are unusual and great fun. There are small electric ones, big, extra-long ones, brightly-colored ones, and a few cars that do not look like cars at all. One car even drives on water!

Mini Cooper

Mini Cooper

The Mini Cooper is a little car, so it is easy to park in cities. It can travel at 126 miles (202 km) an hour, which is fast for such a small vehicle.

Ariel Atom

This car looks like a racing car but it can also travel on normal roads. It has no roof or doors so you can see inside it.

Hummer H2

Stretch Limos

There is space for about 16 passengers in this Hummer, and people have parties in these cars. Some stretch limousines are pink, like the Lincoln Town Car below!

Lincoln Town Car

Which fun car has no roof?

Can you point to?

triangle

circle

letters

lights

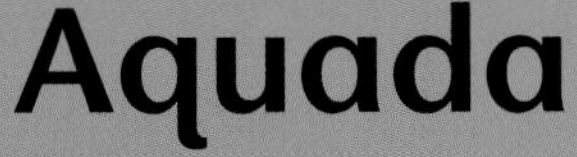

Electric car

Electric Cars

An electric car does not use gasoline. It uses rechargeable batteries. These cars are cheap to run and they do not pollute the atmosphere.

Aquada

This car can drive on land and on water. In water, the wheels are hidden inside the car. It is powerful enough to pull a water-skier!

Gibbs Aquada

MOVIE CARS

Cars that are made for the movies look amazing. In the stories, they can often do clever things, like flying through the air and speeding along on water. These cars are specially designed for the movie and usually only a few are made.

cockpit roof

Batmobile

Batmobile

This Batmobile is the car that Batman drives in the movie *Batman Begins*. It has rocket boosters and armor plating.

Batmobile

Fab 1

This is Lady Penelope's car in *Thunderbirds*. It has six wheels and can travel on land, by air, and on water. In the movie, Lady Penelope sits in the back and her butler, Parker, drives the car.

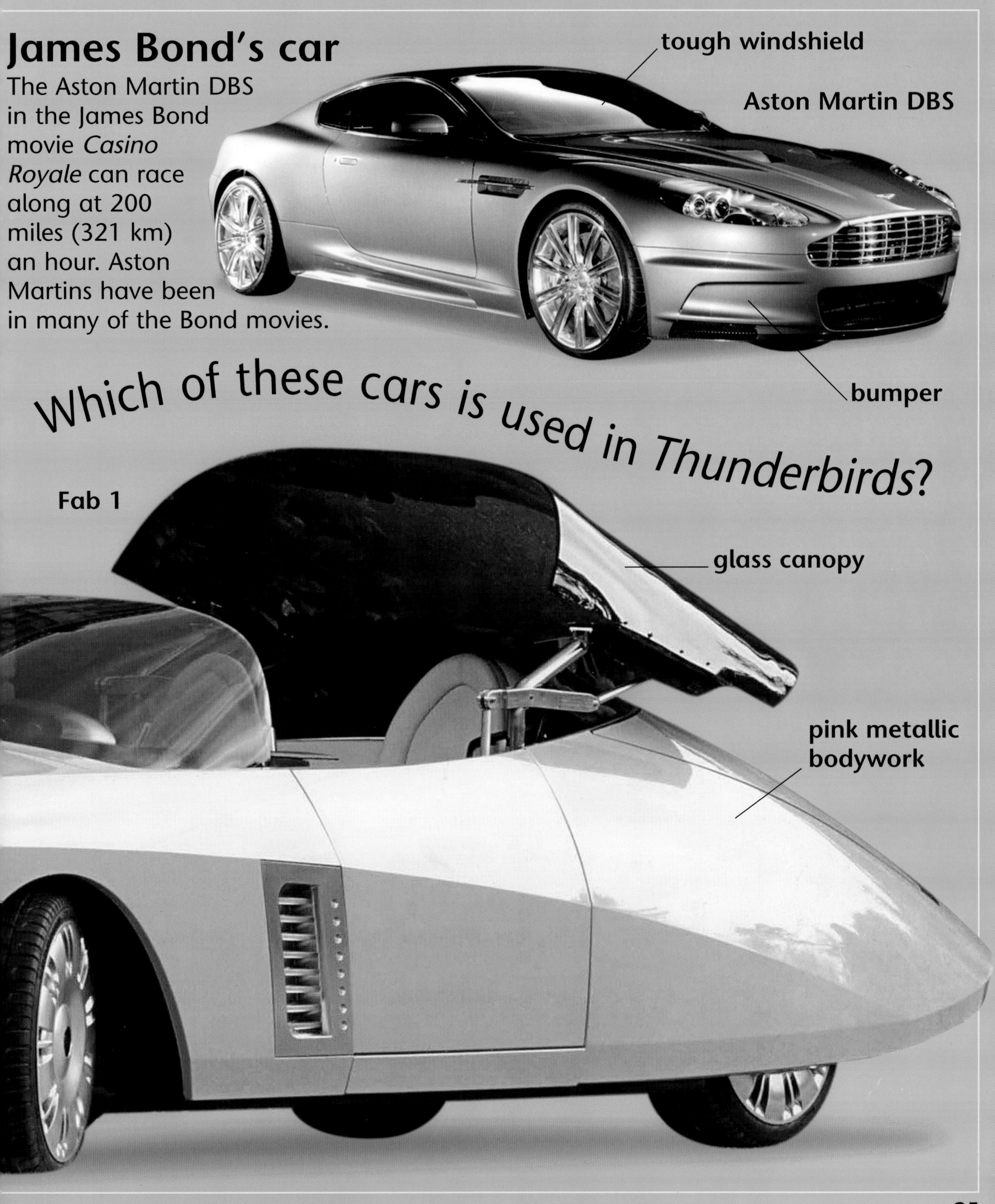

James Bond's car

The Aston Martin DBS in the James Bond movie *Casino Royale* can race along at 200 miles (321 km) an hour. Aston Martins have been in many of the Bond movies.

Which of these cars is used in *Thunderbirds?*

CLASSIC CARS

When very popular cars become old, they are called classic cars. The most exciting and popular cars from the 1960s and 1970s are now classic cars. Some are rare and expensive to buy. One day some of the cars that we drive today may become classics.

Beetle

This popular German car is the Volkswagen Type 1, but it is called the Beetle because of its shape.

Mustang

The Mustang was the first all-American car. It was first built in the 1960s by Ford. Over one millon of these cars were sold in the first 18 months.

Cobra

The AC Cobra was a fast British sports car in the 1960s. It had a big American engine and a lightweight body.

Jaguar

The British E-type Jaguar was the top sports car of the 1960s. It was attractive and very exciting.

Lamborghini

This was one of the top Italian sports cars in the 1970s. Its doors have hinges at the front so they open upward and forward.

Which cars have animal names?

Corvette

This car was built by hand in the 1950s. These fast cars were the first American sports cars.

SUPER-FAST CARS

The fastest car on Earth is called the Thrust SSC. It was the first land vehicle to break the sound barrier, like a supersonic plane. These cars have engines like the ones in a jet plane. People who race record-breaking cars are brave.

Thrust going faster than sound

Thrust SSC

In October 1997, this supersonic car raced at 763 miles (1,227 km) an hour in the Black Rock Desert, Nevada. Thrust SSC has not been beaten yet.

Thrust SSC

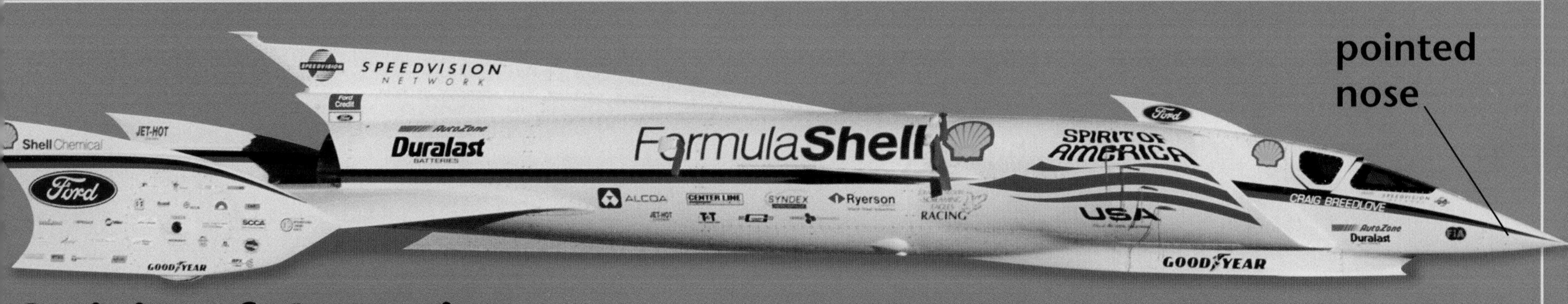

Spirit of America: Sonic Arrow

Spirit of America

This car is nearly 42 feet (13 m) long. It has five wheels and a turbojet engine. It moved at over 650 miles (1,046 km) an hour in the Black Rock Desert in 1996, but then it crashed.

Which is the fastest car of all?

Thrust 2

Thrust 2

This British car has one Rolls-Royce jet engine. Thrust 2 reached a speed of 633 miles (1,018 km) an hour in 1983. It held the Land Speed Record from 1983 to 1997.

Thrust SSC's engines being tested

CARS OF THE FUTURE

Each year thousands of cars are made around the world, especially in the USA, Japan, Germany, and France. Every now and then a brand new type of car is invented. These really modern designs are known as "concept cars."

Smart Crossblade

Smart Car

This little concept car has no roof, doors, or windshield. The Smart car can go up to 85 miles (136 km) an hour.

Morgan Aeromax

Dodge Hornet

This car has six gears and a supercharged engine. Its top speed is 135 miles (217 km) an hour.

Morgan Aeromax

Only 100 of these special Morgans will be built. Inside they have polished wood, and leather that is stitched by hand. The lightweight bodywork is made of aluminum.

Dodge Hornet

Can you point to?

fog lamp

seat

gear stick

Lexus
This two-seater car was built for a film in 2002. There are solar panels on it for recharging the electric engine.
solar panel glass in roof
Lexus Electric Concept Car
body panels that can change color
Inside a Dodge Hornet
Which concept car has no doors?
spoiler
tinted windows
aluminum wheels

LET'S MATCH!

Can you find all the matching pairs on this page?

Which car do you like best?

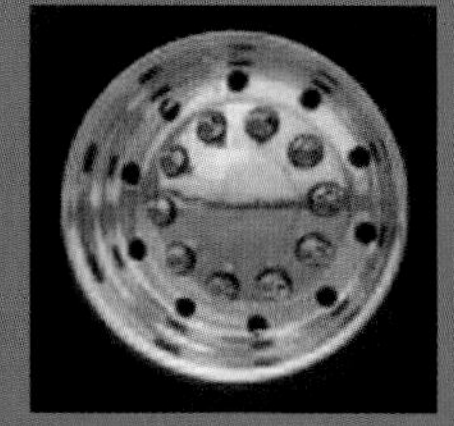

GEARS

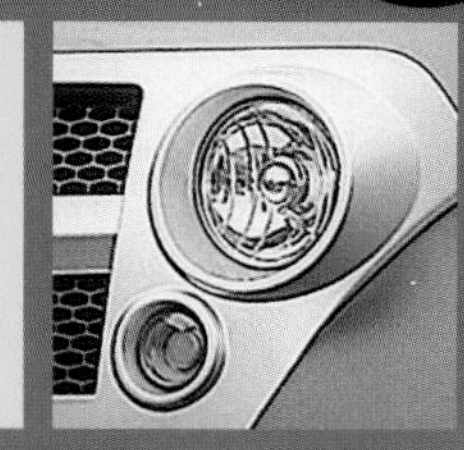

WHEEL

WHEEL

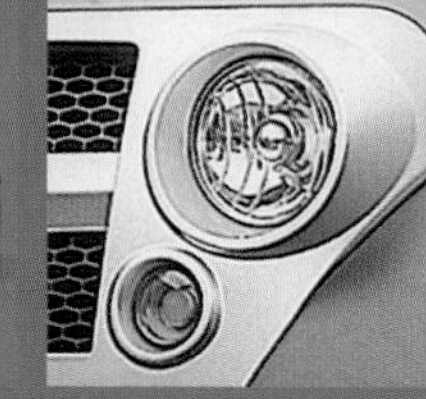

GEARS

TIRE